Tamarins

By Eric Braun and Sandra Donovan

www.steck-vaughn.com

ANIMALS OF THE RAIN FOREST

Copyright © 2002, Steck-Vaughn Company
ISBN 0-7398-4930-1
All rights reserved. No part of this book may be reproduced or utilized in any form or by any means, electronic or mechanical, including photocopying, recording, or by any information storage and retrieval system, without permission in writing from the publisher. Inquiries should be addressed to Copyright Permissions, Steck-Vaughn Company, P.O. Box 26015, Austin, TX 78755.

Library of Congress Cataloging-in-Publication Data
Braun, Eric, 1971-
　　Tamarins/Eric Braun, Sandra Donovan.
　　　　p.cm.—(Animals of the rain forest)
　　Includes bibliographical references (p. 31).
　　Summary: Describes the habitat, physical and social characteristics, and life cycle of the Tamarin monkey, a small endangered mammal that lives in the rain forests of South America.
　　ISBN 0-7398-4684-1
　　ISBN 0-7398-4930-1 (softcover)
　　1. Tamarins—Juvenile literature. [1. Tamarins. 2. Monkeys. 3. Rain forest animals. 4. Endangered species.] I. Title II. Series: Animals of the rain forest.
QL737.P92 B73 2001
599.8'4—dc21

　　　　　　　　　　　　　　　　　　　　　　　　　　　　　　2001019821

Printed and bound in the United States of America
1 2 3 4 5 6 7 8 9 10 WZ 05 04 03 02 01

Photo Acknowledgments
Luiz Claudio Marigo Photography, title page, 6, 16, 18, 22, 24, 26, 28-29
Unicorn Stock Photos/John A. Schakel, Jr., 14
Visuals Unlimited/Ken Lucas Photography, cover
Wildlife Conservation Society/D. Demello, 8; Bill Meng, 11; Diane Shapiro, 12, 21

Content Consultants
Dennis Rasmussen
Director, Primate Refuge and Sanctuary of Panama
Florida State University—Panama

Maria Kent Rowell
Science Consultant
Sebastopol, California

David Larwa
National Science Education Consultant
Educational Training Services
Brighton, Michigan

This book supports the National Science Standards.

Contents

Range Map for Tamarins 4

A Quick Look at Tamarins 5

Tamarins in the Rain Forest 7

What Tamarins Eat 15

A Tamarin's Life Cycle 19

How Are Tamarins Doing? 25

Photo Diagram 28

Glossary 30

Internet Sites, Address, Books to Read 31

Index 32

A Quick Look at Tamarins

What do tamarins look like?
Tamarins are small monkeys. Most are about the size of a squirrel. They have hair, or fur, that covers their whole bodies, except for their faces. Most tamarins are colored dull brown to help them hide in the rain forest trees. Some tamarins have fur that is different colors, such as gold, orange, and red.

Where do tamarins live?
All but one kind of tamarin lives in the rain forests of South America. The Rufous naped tamarin does not live there. It lives in Panama, a part of Central America.

Do tamarins have any enemies?
Yes. Owls, jungle cats, and wild dogs will hunt and eat tamarins. So will snakes, hawks, and eagles.

Tamarins are monkeys that live in rain forest trees.

Tamarins in the Rain Forest

Tamarin monkeys are mammals. A mammal is a warm-blooded animal with a backbone. Warm-blooded animals have a body temperature that stays the same when it is hot or cold outside. The scientific name for the tamarin family is Callitrichidae (kal-uh-TREE-kuh-day).

Tamarins are important to life in the rain forest. A rain forest is a warm place where many different types of trees and plants grow close together and a lot of rain falls. Tamarins eat many kinds of rain forest fruits. Some of the seeds from the fruits leave their bodies as waste. Waste is what the body does not use or need from food that has been eaten. As the monkeys move through the forest, they spread the seeds to new places. New plants grow from the seeds.

▲ This saddle-back tamarin monkey is balancing on a branch in the rain forest.

Kinds of Rain Forest Tamarins

There are several species of tamarin monkeys. A species is a group of animals or plants most closely related to each other in the scientific classification system. The scientific classification system is a way to group and label living things.

Did you know that tamarins use sounds and smells to protect their families? They rub a scent from their bodies onto tree limbs to claim their homes. That way other tamarins will stay away. When they hear enemies, they make loud noises to scare them off.

It helps people study and understand animals and plants.

Most tamarin species look very much alike. Some of their fur color is different. Most are about the size of a squirrel. All but one kind of tamarin lives in the rain forests of South America. The Rufous naped tamarin does not live there. It lives in Panama, a part of Central America. Different species live in different countries.

Another kind of tamarin is the cotton-top tamarin. Their name comes from the white hair that sticks straight up on their heads. They live in the rain forest in Columbia.

Some other kinds of tamarins are the saddle-back tamarin and the pied bare-faced tamarins. There are also emperor tamarins. They have long mustaches and live in Brazil, Peru, and Bolivia. Almost all tamarins are **endangered**.

Where Tamarins Live

Tamarins live in the rain forest because they need the many plants and animals there in order to survive. Each species lives in one rain forest and usually does not ever meet other kinds of tamarins. Emperor tamarins and saddle-back tamarins sometimes live together.

The most important thing that tamarins need from the rain forest is food. There, they find fruits, nuts, and insects to eat. They also find plenty of water to drink.

Rain forest plants and trees are useful to tamarins to help them escape from predators. Predators are animals that hunt other animals and eat them. The animals that predators hunt and eat are called prey. To get away from predators, tamarins move quickly from tree to tree. They can also hide in the trees by staying still and blending in with their background.

Tamarins travel through the rain forest in groups of four or five. Each group has one female, one or two males, and their young. Older tamarins carry the young on their backs when they travel.

▲ **This golden-headed lion tamarin is peeking out of the tree hole where it sleeps.**

At night, the groups sleep together in holes of trees or in tangles of vines and leaves. This makes it hard for predators to find them.

▲ The cotton-topped tamarin was named for the white hair on its head.

What Tamarins Look Like

Tamarins are small monkeys. Most are less than 1 foot (30 cm) tall without counting their tails. The tails can be up to 17 inches (43 cm) long.

Tamarins weigh between 1 and 2 pounds (450 and 900 g). Most lion tamarins weigh about

2 pounds (900 g). Cotton-top tamarins weigh about 1 pound (450 g).

Tamarins have hair, or fur, that covers their whole bodies, except for their faces. This makes their faces and large eyes stand out.

Most tamarins are a dull brown color to help them hide in the rain forest trees. Some tamarins have very bright colors. The golden lion tamarin has bright, golden-orange hair. The black-faced lion tamarin has black hair around its face. The cotton-top tamarin has white hair on top of its head.

Like most monkeys, tamarins' hands and feet are long and thin. They can easily wrap them around tree branches. Their thumbs can move from side to side. People can also move their thumbs from side to side. This kind of thumb is called opposable.

Tamarins have long, pointed claws on their hands. They use them to dig for food under tree bark.

These tamarins are looking in each other's hair for insects to eat.

What Tamarins Eat

Tamarins are **omnivores**. This means they eat both plants and animals. From plants, tamarins eat fruits, seeds, and nuts. Most of these are small enough to put in their mouths and swallow whole. They also eat large fruits, including bananas and oranges. When they find these, they use their claws to peel them.

Tamarins also eat insects, spiders, bird eggs, small lizards, small tree frogs, and small snakes. These give them protein, a substance they need to stay healthy. They use their pointed claws to dig insects and other small animals out of tree bark.

Sometimes tamarins eat ticks and small insect eggs that they find in the fur of other tamarins. Each group spends part of the day looking through each other's fur for these eggs and ticks.

This tamarin is eating fruit during mast fruiting season.

Finding Food

Tamarins spend most of their day traveling in groups, looking for food. They often find food in and under the small plants that grow on rain forest trees. These plants are called **bromeliads**, and the trees they grow on are called **host** trees. Bromeliads form small cups that hold water and insects for tamarins to drink and eat.

Depending on the season, it can be easier or harder for tamarins to find food. Food is harder to find during the dry season in the rain forest. During the wet season, there is more food growing, and so it is easier to find.

Mast Fruiting

Sometimes it is easy for tamarins to find fruit to eat. This is because of **mast fruiting**. Mast fruiting happens when many trees in a large area produce a lot of fruit at the same time. This happens about every three to seven years. During this time, tamarins eat a lot of fruit.

After mast fruiting, there are many months when it is hard to find fruit. During this time, tamarins eat insects.

Male and female tamarins live together in small groups.

A Tamarin's Life Cycle

Tamarins are old enough to mate by the time they are two years old. A female usually lives in a group with one or two males. Once a year, she will mate with one or more of the males. Females usually have young once a year.

Young are usually born about four to five months after mating. They are almost always born in November or December. Scientists think this might be because food is easiest to find then. They think the tamarins have adapted to have their young when more food is available to feed them.

Females almost always have twins. Once in a while, a female will give birth to either one or three young. The young weigh about 1.5 ounces (43 g) at birth.

Raising Young

Mothers and fathers both take care of their young. Fathers carry their young on their backs. Mothers **nurse** their young every two to three hours. Nursing is when a mother feeds her young milk that she makes in her body. Most mammals produce milk to nurse their young.

When tamarins are about six months old, they start to take care of themselves. But they still live with their families for about another year. During this time, they help take care of new young. Sometimes they carry them on their backs. Scientists think this is how young tamarins learn how to care for their own young.

A female stays with her family for about 18 months. Then she leaves to find a mate. She will live in a family group with a male and their young. Sometimes the group will have more than one adult male. There is almost always only one adult female in each group.

A male stays with his mother and father until he is about two years old. Then he leaves to find a mate. Tamarins can live more than 20 years.

This mother tamarin is carrying her young through the trees.

▲ This group of tamarins is grooming each other as they rest in the shade.

What Is a Tamarin's Day Like?

Tamarins sleep at night and spend most of the day traveling through the rain forest trees. They travel to look for food, to avoid their enemies, and to keep track of other groups of tamarins.

Tamarins are busiest in the morning, when groups travel together looking for food. They might do this in the morning because at that time it is cooler in the rain forest.

Tamarins are always trying to keep away from their predators. Owls, jungle cats, and wild dogs will hunt and eat tamarins.

In the early afternoons, groups rest under the layer of leaves of rain forest trees and plants to keep themselves cool. This is the hottest part of the day in the rain forest. After resting, tamarins **groom** each other. They do this by looking through one another's fur for ticks and small insect eggs. When they find eggs and ticks, they eat them. They do this to stay healthy and to clean themselves.

Sleeping

In the late afternoon, groups begin to look for one of the several trees they use to sleep in. They move from tree to tree so predators cannot find them easily. Most tamarins sleep about 30 to 60 feet (10 to 20 m) above the ground.

A tamarin family sleeps together in a hole in a tree or in a tangle of vines or leaves. They sleep with the youngest ones in the middle, to keep them safe. They also sleep with their arms, legs, and tails drawn into their bodies.

This mustached tamarin is in danger of becoming extinct.

How Are Tamarins Doing?

Almost all tamarins are in danger of becoming extinct. Extinct means that there are no more of that species of animal living.

The main reason that tamarins are in danger is because the rain forest is disappearing. Tamarins are losing their habitat. A habitat is place where an animal or plant usually lives. At one time, rain forests covered much of Panama and South America. Then people began cutting down the forests to build houses, towns, and roads. Many tamarins are killed by cars and trucks when the monkeys try to cross the roads.

Today, farmers cut down the forests to make more room for crops and animals. Other people cut down the forests to get firewood and lumber. Now there is very little rain forest left in South America.

▲ These scientists are releasing this tamarin into the wild rain forest.

Tamarins in the Future

Hunters trap tamarins and sell them as pets. To protect tamarins, governments have made hunting against the law in most countries where tamarins live.

Some scientists take male and female tamarins out of the rain forest. They bring them to zoos to **breed** them. Breeding means to keep animals and plants to produce more of them. Scientists do this so there will be more tamarins in the future. In the rain forest, the tamarins are in danger of being killed before they can mate. Young tamarins in zoos are protected so they can grow up to mate.

Tamarins Moving to the Rain Forest

Most tamarins born in zoos are not able to survive in the wild. They have not learned how to hunt for food or how to protect themselves from predators.

Scientists try to teach these tamarins how to take care of themselves in the rain forest. This is called **re-introduction**. Scientists have to teach them where to look for food. They also teach them how to keep away from their enemies.

People who try to save tamarins hope that breeding and re-introducing them will lead to more tamarins in the future. Many people understand that tamarins are important to life in the rain forest. They must teach other people what they know. Together, people of all ages can help keep tamarins alive in their rain forest homes for a very long time.

Glossary

breed (BREED)—when people keep animals and plants to help produce more of them

bromeliads (broh-MEE-lee-uhds)—small plants that grow on rain forest trees

endangered (en-DAYN-jurd)—in danger of becoming extinct

groom (GROOM)—to look through the fur of another animal to clean it

host (HOHST)—an animal or plant upon which another living thing grows

mast fruiting (MAST FROOT-ing)—a time during which many trees in the rain forest produce much fruit

nurse (NURSS)—when a mother feeds her young milk made inside her body

omnivore (OM-nuh-vor)—an animal that eats both plants and other animals

re-introduction (ree-in-truh-DUHK-shuhn)—to return an animal to its natural habitat after teaching it how to take care of itself in the wild

Internet Sites

Project Tamarin Web Site
http://www.selu.com/bio/cottontop/gallery/index.html

Wild Ones Animal Index: Lion Tamarin
http://www.thewildones.org/Animals/tamarin.html

Useful Address

Tamarin Exhibit
Central Park Wildlife Center
830 Fifth Ave.
New York, NY 10021

Books to Read

Ancona, George. *The Golden Lion Tamarin Comes Home.* New York: Macmillan, 1994.

Costain, Meredith. *Golden Lion Tamarin Monkeys.* Littleton, MA: Sundance, 2000.

Index

Bolivia, 9
Brazil, 9
breed, 27
bromeliads, 17

Central America, 5, 9
claws, 13, 15

endangered, 9
extinct, 25

groom, 22, 23

habitat, 25
host, 17

mammal, 7, 20
mast fruiting, 16, 17
mating, 19

nurse, 20

omnivore, 15

Panama, 5, 9, 25
Peru, 9
predator, 10, 11, 23, 27
prey, 10
protein, 15

re-introduction, 27

scientist, 19, 20, 26, 27
sleep, 11, 22, 23
South America, 5, 9, 25

warm-blooded, 7
waste, 7

zoo, 27